GATOR, GATOR, GATOR!

by Daniel Bernstrom

Illustrated by Frann Preston-Gannon

HARPER

An Imprint of HarperCollinsPublishers

ISBN 978-0-06-246330-2

The artist used mixed media and Photoshop
to create the digital illustrations for this book.
Typography by Rachel Zegar

❖

21 22 RTLO 10 9 8 7 6 5 4 3 2
First Edition

To Phyllis Root &
Jacqueline Briggs Martin.
Thank you for guiding me on my
picture book adventure!
—D.B.

For my beautiful friends, Alice & Karis.
—F.P.G.

Have you heard about the gator
in the bayou thick with moss?
Granny SAYS his "skin's like nails!"
Says his "temper's hot like sauce!"

He is wider than a school bus
and is longer than a tree.
He is silent like a secret.
No one knows where
he might be.

Do you wanna?

Wanna come?

Do you wanna come and see?

Let's go find that
gator-gator-gator!

Come with me.

Got some rules.
Some directions.
Would you please
pay close attention!

NOT A HAND IN THE SWAMP.
NOT A FOOT O'ER THE SIDE.
DO NOT JUMP ON ANY LOG.
DO NOT GO FOR ANY RIDE.

Oh, one more. . . . Don't jump in!

Don't you **dare** go for a swim!

Or I promise — see you later.

You with Mr. Alligator!

Over yonder!
Near the shore!

See that lily-padded patch?
See him hiding in the middle,
waiting for a tasty snack.

That's sure him.

Don't believe me?
I'd sure bet you my pink socks.

There he is!
Don't you see him?

Oh, sorry . . .
just a fox.

Oh, sorry . . .
just a **snake**.

Oh, sorry . . .
just a rat.

Over yonder!
In that swamp!

See that shadow black as night?
How it hides below the duckweed,
near the reeds and out of sight?

That's sure him!
Don't believe me?
I'd sure bet a million bucks!

There he is!
You don't see him?

Oh, I'm sorry . . .
just some **ducks**.

It's sure quiet . . .
awful quiet. . . .
Don't dare move a muscle, friend.
I sure swear that gator's out here. . . .

WAIT!

Did you rock the boat just then?

You know what I've been thinkin'?
Best leave well enough alone.
I ain't scared.
And I ain't chicken.

BUMP! BUMP!

Was that you, friend?
Don't say no.

Over
yonder,

see them eyes,
how they twinkle in the sun?
There he is!
Please believe me!

Watch out!
Watch out!

Here he comes!

Water's whirring.
See it stirring.
Better start that motor quick!

We should hurry!
Time's a-wastin'!

Chugga

Chugga

Click.

Click.

Click.

Try again!
Gator's coming!

Vroom Vroom Vroom! NOW! Go! Go!

Go! Hurry! Hurry! Move it! Move it! Move it!

We're not stopping!
No! No! No!

Find land!

Dock boat!

Come on back and HIDE!

Do you see our friend the gator?

Do you see him in the moss?

I just know he's out there somewhere—
monster gators don't get lost.

He is close by—I can feel him.
And I know where he might be.

But I need a friend,
a friend like you . . .
to come back out with me.

So . . .
Do you wanna?
Wanna come?
Do you wanna come and see?
Let's go find that
gator-gator-gator!

Come with me!